MW01514393

As Do I

:(

Part One

Myth, Magic, Madness

"Poems to make you believe again"

Colby

I hope magic finds you Jean, everywhere you go but especially in the places you have yet to look. —Colby

Copyright © 2020 by Colby Trotter

All rights reserved. No part of this book may be reproduced or used in any manner without written permission of the copyright owner except for the use of quotations in a book review. For more information, address:

ColbyTrotterBooks@gmail.com

FIRST EDITION

www.colbytrotterbooks.com

A word from a friend

"As Do I" is a blend of Cheerfully Melancholic poetry and micro-poetry. Cheerfully Melancholic is something I coined to describe the nature of breathing sorrow and exhaling joy with such ease that it becomes difficult to identify where one ends and the other begins. Everything within this book is filled with that sentiment.

It will encourage the reader to come down to a level at which their darkest sides reside while simultaneously lifting them to match the transcendent tone found within each theme.

This process will gently massage the readers understanding of their own happiness and the journey we all share to borrow a little more. The three themes of the book each seek to tell the story of this one adventure out and within from their own unique perspectives.

I hope in the end, it leaves you at least once saying that "I feel that too" or "As do I." The journey to borrow a little extra happiness might be your own but it's nice to have some company along the way.

Your Cheerfully Melancholic Friend,

- Colby

Myth, Magic, Madness

Because I want to make you feel things.

Things so intense and unique

~~that they leave you wondering~~

if anyone, anywhere has ever been able to

wrap a string of letters around it

and speak its name.

Thank you for sharing

in my ups and downs

which are what make me

so consistently Cheerfully Melancholic.

May the sad moments

help you find the light.

May the happy moments

remind you of your own.

I wrote this for you. I wrote this for me. I

wrote this for each person

I couldn't save and each one

that will surely come after.

Statements that should always

remain unpunctuated

speak it as a promise to never stop

I believe In you

I love you

I miss you

There are thousands upon thousands

of quotes about life

when it has lost its luster.

Where are the quotes about

waking up and realizing

how delicious the air tastes

when you left your window open

on the first crisp night before fall?

Where are the quotes about biting into an

orange after brushing your teeth and just

how intense that flavor is?

Where are the quotes about holding

someone's hand for the first time

: (: 2

and that look you share after?

I guess in a world where people can find

a million reasons to be dismal,

today I just want to focus on one that

can captivate the day with its vibrance.

———————————————————

: (: 3

My letter never arrived

but I found magic

nevertheless

:(: 4

It's an old variety of magic

that keeps this page from burning away

when it came from a soul set aflame

Even if my Name is to be worn away

by history's hand

may my voice

never cease to ring

in your ears

:(: 6

Speak it aloud

Is it you?

If not, I hope you say something else.

I don't think that you ever quite forget

what made you first believe in magic

: (: 8

I'm not the hand nor the foot

but that little voice

you can't remember

until you have already forgotten.

That is where I will always be found.

: (: 9

Laugh until your cheeks burn red

till your chest feels as if it will cave in

but most importantly

do so until you forget

what you were laughing at

in the first place

Embrace your darkest sides.

They can do less harm when held close.

Our thoughts orbit within

the universes we create

A fairy tale for all of those people

who haven't had one written

in their honor yet.

Here's to the lost

but not wanting to be found.

Here's to the broken

who learn to mend themselves

but most of all here's to those

who are single and yet complete.

: (: 13

Go where the magic is

: (: 14

I take my nuance

like my bourbon, neat

What is magic but a way of describing that

tempo that our hearts beat

in sync with?

What is magic but the tune to which a

lover's breathing moves to?

What is magic but the reason we woke up

today and another did not?

What is magic but what we call it

when we give it a name?

I feed my fire

with the thoughts

of what could have been

because I need the warmth now

and not then

I know it to be true that

if you fight the current long enough you

will drown

and

we think our souls are any different?

: (: 18

I may never have anything nice

but I can tell you firsthand

how far the string can be pulled

and describe the way

the fabric puckers as it's done

Flame not only fills darkness

but consumes it

: (: 20

Embrace your shadow.

After all, it's never once left your side.

Chase your shadow even if it takes you

past the second star to the right

and straight on till morning.

Chase it today

Chase it tomorrow

but

Chase it especially then

When the ocean has been mapped

and every star catalogued

perhaps then

we will be properly equipped

to explore the soul

As the moon uses darkness

to embrace you goodnight

so the sun will be there

to kiss you good morning

: (: 24

From time to time

I read of something divine

But not in the way

that one might

consistently decipher a line

I read of this and I read of that

My soul can't help but to crack

Pressure building from

what I have poured into

but can never track

If you drink sunshine

you can't help but be bright

That tingling in my soul

as an idea takes hold

I breathe in savoring the way it fills

goosebumps rise

to the surface of my skin

and the idea becomes reality

as I exhale

Stories are like pharmaceuticals

in that they can literally alter your

composition and chemistry

but the difference being

that the effects are most often

permanent

While true we may never discover that Old

Magic

You know the kind?

The one that leaves you both breathless

and under the impression

that the laws of even gravity

no longer apply?

What a wonderful time we will

share though, simply telling stories

in the sunshine until we forget what we

were searching for in the first place.

I'm not sure if it was written in the stars

but check for me from time to time

because I know it will be

I don't mean to look into connections

and conversations so deeply

but I just can't help but pick up

the bits & crumbs and be curious

where they lead.

Sometimes I think my mind

assigns meaning to the arbitrary

often I really value

this connection to connections.

I feel like it's almost

a superpower of sorts.

I can see the strings that attach things

and give those small threads

:(: 31

with the proper lighting and handling

a gentle tug.

They have a certain importance to me

while others may think

they are too small to notice.

I truly believe

that the most beautiful things

are the ones that are easily overlooked.

The ones we have to hunt for.

The mystery behind the magic that makes

a moment out of a minute.

If I'm honest

the wide eyed youth of my past

would be upset

with the man I have become

and I mourn for his feelings.

The tragic truth though

I just hope the frail old man

that is my future

can crack a proud smile

knowing what's to come.

It's not so much

that you make me believe in magic

as wonder how I have lived

this long without it

: (: 34

What if every path

I have ever thought about taking was just

a new character in the making

I yearn for what I can feel

but not yet see

and for this reason

I will pursue what can be held

but never touched

It would be lovely to have another

note me amongst the pages of history

in italicized typed 12 font

but if not

the world will just have to deal

with my manic scrawl

: (: 37

Never miss a chance

to light the torch of another

you do not know

when you may need the favor in return

One can rewrite their scars

They are just reminders of a story

but how it is written and told

is entirely up to you.

One can rewrite their scars

this much has always been true.

: (: 39

It's perplexing how the rain

can wash away even the most

jarring of sounds from a day.

The droplets cease to fall

and like magic

a clean pervading silence follows.

: (: 40

Those who think

they are worth remembering

probably are

The skill of a liar

is not in how well they can fool others

but rather in how splendidly

they can fool themselves

: (: 42

You reach for a glass of water

Each time you bring it to your lips it

contains something else.

That's what loneliness is like

any of these things

could normally satiate you

but you're left wanting

because you can only focus

on what you do not have.

Two people listen to very similar radios

but are tuned into different stations.

They may share a love

for the radio itself

but when the silence begins

they will have nothing to fill it with.

May you find people

who can fill a silence without speaking

regardless of the stations

you each choose.

: (: 44

Perhaps sanity is simply

about the number of strings

you still have left intact

There's something almost rhythmic about the temporary way people convene as individuals to create a crowd. These obscure pieces can be played by themselves and contain varied levels of organization and beauty. The crescendo occurs though when these pieces are played alongside one another in a soul vibrating harmony. It's the kind of symphony that you can never repeat but always capture.

The line between normal and crazed

shouldn't be flirted with

but erratically pirouetted over

Energy is like water, in that

the flow can be guided

It's a lifelong effort to remove

anything that obstructs the flow

I have this mental image of a faucet

I'm able to control the temperature

the strength of the stream

or whether it flows at all.

:(: 48

Soak up the tragedy of today

for it's the tale of tomorrow

<u>For you, Mr. Fitzgerald</u>

Show me a tragedy

and I will write you

A Hero

:(: 50

Lock obstacles and objectives

in a room with your manic flames

and watch as they twist and melt

into nonexistence

Mania is a lot like fire

while lovely beyond compare

it can burn up everything around it

if left untamed

I behold beauty

and let it wash away

the grit of the day.

Nothing cleans under your fingernails

and between your toes

like a lather of lovely lyrics

or a hot stream of simple sentences.

When I feel the fog creeping around

and threatening to smother me

I flood my mind

with every beautiful thing

I know for sure to be true

Don't give it another inch

for to lose even an inch today

could mean a life tomorrow.

The fog mustn't ever win.

I believe in you

please

Measure your words carefully

but not so much so

that you hang yourself with the tape

I just don't think

things ever

really end

After a piece of art is produced

it is displayed

after a novel is written

it is read

When I think about what of me

when I am dead

maybe the pieces I left in another's head?

Just because you're the only one dancing

doesn't mean there's not music playing

The moment

we accept the impossible

we open ourselves up

to the greatest stories of all

Something has changed within me

it's as if

someone has turned the tune up

and raised the lights

Weather is an indicator of climate but

don't be fooled by a single forecast.

Hurricanes occur within tropical places.

The sun can warm your skin in even

the most frigid of its phases

and we all carry

a large number of faces

who we are and what we see

may leave very different traces

: (: 60

Trace a circle

around the perimeter of your soul

and expel anything

that doesn't fit

within YOUR boundaries

You don't need every detail

to tell the story.

Focus on one,

it can be as small

as the way a grain of sand

feels between two of your toes.

It can be as large

as the political climate

in a civilization of your design.

Don't let the noise and clutter

in your mind, distract.

In fact

subtract it and keep subtracting

: (: 62

until you have nothing

but that one detail left.

Then work on the next.

This is how change occurs:

slowly, intentionally, and methodically.

Don't tell them what you will do

show them the blisters laid open

and rubbed ruby raw

as you hold up your hand

to the light of a day

it has not yet known

Sometimes Heroes aren't the ones

we see when we look to the sky

but the ones speaking beside us

when we have forgotten the sound

of our own voices

in that sky

with that hero

who never came.

: (: 65

Don't Miss Your Mark

If life gives you a stage

either play your fucking part

or vacate the space

because this much has always been true

The Show Must Go On

Architects will create buildings

from their very thoughts

engineers will build those buildings

as they know best

Doctors with their measure

will keep those men alive

who dream up buildings

and those who build them

Without a Poet though

you will never know

why, you

created it

built it

: (: 67

kept the thought

or the man

alive long enough to do so.

————————————————————

Intermission

:(: 69

-Sincerely, Amelia L. Blaine

A lovely thought indeed. We all have it within us to make time stand still. If that's not the most magical concept you have read of today, I would very much like to borrow your book. Your life is so significant that time herself forgets to breathe, and for a moment ceases to move forward even if just for a moment. Why not? What if time is more sentimental and romantic than even we are?

Her seconds, a gingerly push forward, always forward. Her minutes our sweet encouragement that we can make it to the next one. Her hours, her serene song detailing the stories of the minutes had and the ones still to come. Her days just a well worn chapter of a favorite book.

Time being the owner and collector of a great many works, it still amazes me that my own would be amongst them. Maybe your work is one that shows wear from being read and reread like any

great book should. Is it possible your character is

actually one of her all time favorites? She

celebrated your successes and mourned your losses

from the first chapter to the last.

Maybe she just wants you to give her a reason

to take your collective breath away. A magic so

innate and of the oldest kind that a minute can

transform into a moment and even if for the most

fleeting second, time stands still long enough to

revel and let it wash over the both of you.

The Philosophers Stone

I am both chemist and alchemist.

I will bottle these happy thoughts

for you today.

When a time comes

that the curse takes hold

and you can no longer move

I will press that vial to your lips

to make sure

you remember

what you are forever cursed to forget.

I will turn your leaden sorrow

into a kind of gold

: (: 72

that will always leave you feeling wealthy

and worthy.

This I promise you

as I am both chemist and alchemist.

_____

I know of no greater magic

than that which gave us the power

to keep breathing

once our mind

had given up

: (: 74

Watch as I cast this vision

for the future before you

It's not mere poetry

but a manifestation

of everything to come

Only then will you know

it to be true

a magician you are

and have always been

: (: 75

5. Not all parts were written equal

4. Villains are never born

but always written in, after

3. If you can't find something written

maybe you're the one to write it

2. Live a life worthy of the stories

you have lived thus far

anything short of that

is just bad writing

1. Be Better Written

: (: 76

Prometheus Continued...

Happiness is a flame that you steal from

the gods themselves.

This raw power is kept

in the darkest corners of existence.

In order to gain it we must lose

entire parts of ourselves

and endure a great deal of scarring.

Once held, though, it can bring light

to the darkest night and warm

even the chillest of bone.

While eternal in nature,

it can be whispered out of existence

: (: 77

with the slightest of breaths.

Protect it for the dark corners

do not forget

and it's the only thing

that can protect you in return.

Find Your Frequency

Singing in harmony with your soul

will not only alter your tone

but forever change your life

Rings And Things

I am molten gold

in that you can see my value

but it's anyone's guess

what I will solidify into.

Perhaps that's my fate

to symbolize something special

to each of you

frozen

in both celebration and solidarity.

Do me this one favor though?

Love with the potential I present?

Choose something beautiful

: (: 80

to caress your neck

or gently squeeze your wrist

when the reason

you first adorned me

has long ago faded.

———————————————————

Revolution is found

in the smile that spites the tear

I binge on poetry and you

because some things

were never meant for moderation

: (: 83

Names are important

we either

live up to them or in spite of them

: (: 84

Who will you be

when the curtain closes?

How long will it take

for you to break character?

:(: 85

We are all actors and artists

some are better compensated than others

but all of us are starving

for a shot of lead or light

and not necessarily in that order

: (: 86

Just because the door doesn't open

when you try it the first time

doesn't mean it's not your door

to walk through.

Some people are born with the keys

others, a sledgehammer

and I just can't find my fucking keys.

: (: 87

I think people should take

at least one day a week

and watch the sun rise

If for no other reason

than to see

how our lives are reflected

in natural processes

: (: 88

Asking for a Friend

Can conversations be caffeinated?

Bad decisions are like any seasoning

they should be sprinkled

in for spice

to avoid leaving a dish bland

but if used in excess

can render even the best of cuisine

inedible

: (: 90

It's not that I'm necessarily

meant to be someone

but that I already am

The reason you don't fit

into the puzzle

is because you're the one

putting it together

I never could figure out

what I wanted to be

when I grew up

so I told stories of the people

I could have

and could not

have been

as a result I never did

: (: 93

You can live your whole life

for something

but dying for it

still doesn't make it true

Worse than Forgetting

We will never remember

what was not first

completed

If the life you want

is out of reach

either stretch or get your hands dirty and

create it

from the clay of potential around you

There's something

inexplicably intoxicating

about Novel people and New places

It's all the nourishment

I have ever needed

: (: 97

We may share a page, perhaps even

a whole chapter or two

but the book of your life

will never share an author

: (: 98

May your soul remain soluble

Souls are like salt

in that they can both disappear

into the solvents of life

but also outlast them

Isn't it interesting

when someone

speaks matter of factly

without uttering

a single honest syllable

I wonder where I will wander

wander with the wind.

Wind the clock of my life so that I may

never go wanting.

Wanting nothing more or less than what

the whimsical can provide.

A whim in which day dreams don't wilt.

Wilt I will

but write of us so that we may in time

grow to be immortal.

For You Hamlet

To be content or have content

that is the question

I may never be a sure thing

but you can be sure

I will always bet on me

If the number of fucks is finite

like you say

may each one be filled

with fun, friends, and yes

occasionally even something frivolous

I need to have

autonomy, inspiration

and the time to tirelessly pursue

what ever captivates my heart

in that particular hour

How much of our lives

are created out of consistency

(convenience) rather than in spite of it

Feeling connected

is much less about

the actual connection

than it is about

the expectation of being so

: (: 107

I like being alone

sometimes

but coincidentally

I never like

feeling as though I am

:(: 108

The key to a well written character

is surrounding yourself

with lots of material

You may not always love

where you are in life

but may you always love

who you are

what you are doing

whom it is with

and the direction

in which you're headed

I feel unstoppable

not because

of what I have

but because

of what I do not need

Seek to write a better story

than the one

that was written for you

I just love the way

words embrace me and pull me close

Nothing says

conformity like a cemetery

If you need but one example

of humanities innate brilliance

all you must ask is

"Why?"

Say yes to adventure

especially when it's wrapped

in such a

serendipitous manner

Be wary of people

who ask you questions

they either want

something from you

or in the truly tragic cases

it's you that they want

Laugh just to fill the silence

smile when there's not a soul around

dance in the rain

because you damn well please

I'm filled by the words

of those spoken before me

and intrigued by those

that in consequence

will come after

I love the idea

that my story

is a book in progress

If for no other reason

than the world needs

a few more cliches

Surround yourself with people

who think you're funny.

There's no medicine in the world

like a laugh

that leaves you crying

It might seem foolish

to equate the placing of miles on a soul

with nourishment

but then again

I have gone without one

but never the other

I am meant to be someone

in the same way

I am meant to eat breakfast

There's nothing that really says

I have to

but I feel hungry nevertheless

I think anyone who aspires to write

should make an effort

of feeling lonely

at least once.

If for no other reason

it teaches the importance of well written

supporting characters.

Some people know

more about their favorite characters

than they do themselves

and that makes me sad

They were written

in such a way

that I'm still not convinced

it wasn't fiction

What if the best thing about you

is something you haven't discovered

or worse, never do

What if just by asking

bigger questions

you welcome bigger answers

and as a direct result

smaller problems

Fact can become fiction

and fiction can become fact

but for now that's enough of that

It's how you treat

those who have wronged you

that defines a character

Language is an ancient tool

we have passed down

to capture and describe frequencies

that carry inherent meaning.

We have given them

each a syllable, a structure, a name

so now they are.

: (: 131

I'm too old

to believe in fairytales

but young enough

to not let that stop me

My Mountain

I see my mountain

and it grows

increasingly more magnificent

with each step.

It's time to start hiking

as if night will set, for it surely will.

I'm packed and I have set my course,

all that's left

is the sweat to bead,

the blisters to rub raw,

and the exhaustive glory

of placing one foot

in front of the other.

———————————————————————

The Best Endings, Don't

:(:

The Journey Continues...
In Part Two

AS DO I

AS DO I

LOVE, LUST, LOSS

The Journey to borrow a
continues with this sequ
Magic, Madness." Colby
role as a Cheerfully Mela
best and worst of emotio
ravel the knots left withi
and lusted

"Passion looks l
you should wear

Colby makes a living
inspiring, and healing
he breathes into life.
of the flame. Follow hi

Instagram: @Co
Facebook: @Colby

COLBY TROTTER

About the Author

Colby Trotter graduated from the University of Kentucky and currently lives in Peoria, Illinois. When he is not writing poetry, he spends his time traveling, road cycling, raising a glass of wine with his Pops, creating a new cocktail, or baking something fresh from scratch.

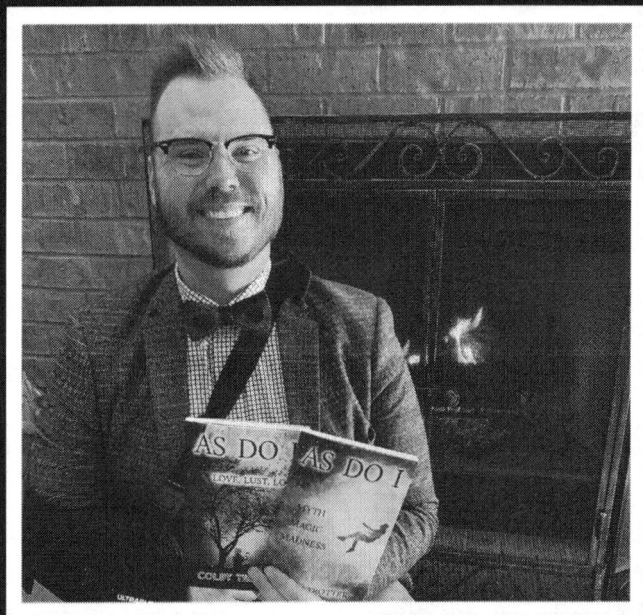

If you enjoyed book one

of the "As Do I" poetry series,

please share your favorite pages

with us and a friend.

Don't forget to check out

book two as well.

: (:

Subscribe

For More Poetry and Book Updates

www.ColbyTrotterBooks.com

Coming Soon

-Sincerely Amelia

"A coming of age story.

One that will remind each of us,

that it's never too late

to not grow up."

Colby Trotter Books

2020: As Do I: Myth, Magic, Madness

2020: As Do I: Love, Lust, Loss

2021: -Sincerely Amelia

I Dedicate This To You

Poppsy & Mummsy

Tomi-Jean

Conner

Kinners

Aunt Pat

Tink

Sierra

Lila

Janie Lou

And many, many more.

Your love and support might be

the best magic of all.

I couldn't have done it without you.

Made in the USA
Columbia, SC
09 June 2021

39583866R00083